The Parable Boat

The Parable Boat

Hannah Main-van der Kamp

October 2010, Sorrento

To Margery,
How great to meet another poetry lover!
Thank you for the encouragement!

May the mystery of poetry always be a delight!

Wolsak and Wynn . Toronto

Hannah

© Hannah Main-van der Kamp, 1999

All rights reserved. No part of this book may be reproduced or transmitted in any form, by any means, electronic or mechanical, without permission in writing from the publisher, except by a reviewer who may quote brief passages in a review. In case of photocopying or other reprographic copying, a licence is required from CANCOPY (Canadian Copyright Licensing Agency), One Yonge Street, Suite 1900, Toronto, ON, CANADA M5E 1E5.

Typeset in Garamond, printed in Canada by
The Coach House Printing Company, Toronto.

Front cover art:: "Wind Prayer", Boat © Peggy Vanbianchi,; photo by Jane Lindley
Cover design: Stan Bevington
Author's photograph: J.R. Main

Some of these poems have previously appeared in the following journals to whose editors the author is grateful: *ARC, Canadian Literature, Christianity and the Arts, Fiddlehead, Grail, Grain, League of Canadian Poets 97, The Malahat Review, Radix, Review for Religious, Rim.Victoria Naturalist, Vox Feminarum.*
The publishers gratefully acknowledge the support of the Canada Council for the Arts for our publishing program.

Wolsak and Wynn Publishers Ltd.
Post Office Box 316
Don Mills, Ontario, Canada M3C 2S7

Canadian Cataloguing in Publication Data

Main-Van Der Kamp, Hannah J.
    The parable boat

Poems.
ISBN 0-919897-66-5

I.   Title.
PS8576.A4937P37 1999   C811'.54   C99-931107-7
PR9199.3.M34P37 1999

For my father, Wolter van der Kamp
1913-1998

"Bless the Lord, O my soul ...
Who coverest thyself with light
As with a garment
Who stretchest out the heavens like a curtain."

Psalm 104

CONTENTS

The parable boat

    Parable Boat   13
    Abundance   14
    How to qualify for membership in the reign of heaven   15
    The sea separates from the dry land   16
    For good   17
    Manicheans   18
    "The law in my members' wars against the law of my mind"   19
    Why prairie barns are red   20
    A light burden   22
    Advent folly   23
    The Guadalupe appears to the Nyman-Marcus shoppers in Arizona   24
    Alone in the house on Christmas Eve with the blessed sacrament   25
    Revelation   26

Adam and Eve in middle age

    Calling   27
    Valentine's Day   28
    Ashes   29
    Skinnydipping   31
    Red-breasted mergansers   32
    Mt Trauberg   33
    A middle-aged couple goes to the beach to neck   34
    "... And whatever Adam called every living thing, that was the name thereof"   35
    Eve tells stories   36
    Conjugal relations   37
    Backbone and foreboding   38
    Hyakataki   39

A north-west Lent

    To the same window again   41
    Five Lenten exercises   43
    Every polarity attracts its opposite   44
    Emptying the hands   45
    The silence that is not silence at all   46
    Long weekend on Mayne Island   47
    Shopless in Seattle   49
    St Basil's Ukrainian Church   50

A lent retreatant travels home   51
Supposing him to be the gardener   52

Into the clearing
Emily Dickinson   53
Pubescence   54
Covenant   55
The priestess' role of botanical illustrator   56
Spring salad   57
Poor Clares   58
Magnolias   59
Manna   60
Membranous space in infant's head at adjacent angles of parietal bones   61
Dowagers   62
Hypo-thyroid waltz   63
Morning, noon and night   64
Hermit's garden   65
Eco-feminist theacosmology   66
Pavarotti takes Watercolour lessons   67
Thieves   68
Setting fire to the earth   69
The eschatology of woe and the eschatology of bliss   70
Avian therapy   71
Watershed   72
What you have always with you   73

Santa Rita Abbey
Who in their right mind   75
Desert Cistercians decide to plant roses   76
The practice of standing still   77
The solemnity of Joseph   78
From my youth they have afflicted me but not prevailed   79
Fluff   80
Encompassed   81
Bread of heaven   82
Bajadas   83
Compline   84

Acknowledgements   87

THE PARABLE BOAT

PARABLE BOAT

Peel the stems of coppiced willow and tie them
into a hull. Rope strips of veined, bleached cow gut
side by side and lash those to the frame.
Tattoo with emblems.

This vessel can sail to the Poles but not to marinas.
This vessel does not do apologetics. It is
the idea of a boat but don't get that into your head.

It will sail with certainty only by the light of comets.
When you step in, you forget your destination.

Do you want stability? You'll have to look for something linear.
Perhaps those who expect a logical way to travel
had better rig up an explicator.

Copper talismans rattle on the staves.
Perishable boat. Lie down in the stern for sleep
and gaze through rips wide enough
to view the Pleiades.

Dolphin mares in the bow waves.
Skin ship, airy basket,
transport me.

ABUNDANCE

Sliced silk hour of predawn. A sliver
of day peeks out, draws back
into a crimson thread.

I drink thin tea, shiver
in the bare grass. An early eagle
wings home, tiny fins in its fists.

Children still replete in their sleep
turn over and return to remnants of rest.
The hungry are filled with small things.

Cerulean tiara crowns
this slight terra firma, magnified
by the pouring out

of restrained light.

HOW TO QUALIFY FOR MEMBERSHIP
IN THE REIGN OF HEAVEN

Compost everything and frequently turn it to air.
That includes your headaches, rashes, your unspent rages.

Children enrolled in narrow rooms need release;
then show them the rest of our place, you know...
Orion's belt, Andromeda, the journeys of planets.

Look into the eyes of animals. It matters.
Can you paint them on cave walls? Search
a secret place where the hermit thrush has gone to die
and flute there.

When grandiose persons try to enlarge by talking,
diminish yourself; mute and honest as an oval stone.

Be alert at the dusk moment when light
turns over. Be there when Venus rises
and at the moon's wake. Your presence
is your membership.

THE SEA SEPARATES FROM THE DRY LAND

Up early, hills beget themselves.
Pewter filaments web water,
waver and dissolve.
Glass petals melt to shore.

Across the bay, a predawn start
at the Dryland Sort. Earthmovers
handle sticks, a choreography of sorts.
What to keep and what to discard.

Moon facing East, backs off.
Sandpipers query their southbound journey
but carry on. Out to the edge of the known world
a kingfisher rattles, does not hesitate.

Tides shift. Between what was
and what is to come, a blue sliver
of pause. It is the morning
of the first day.

FOR GOOD

Crows descend air slopes
slalom down and arrive with a *swoosh*.
They set up their hoarse hollering with nothing
much to say. Nervous in stillness
as we all are.
Would you silence them?

Summer tide drifts over sunburnt flats.
You step into the tepid bath, relax and enter
a patch so icy it makes your eyes bulge.
Quick! Paddle out and rediscover
the bliss of a warm current.
Would you have it otherwise?

Toss on driftwood. Around a beach fire
faces emerge lit up, centered on song.
More wood thrown on; a black belch
of stench. Groan. Creosote debris
intermingled with clean cedar. Would you go
into the dark with zeal to sort firewood?

The countenances shine like converged suns.
Complex smoke scent lingers in clothes.
As for the crows,
especially at dawn, go ahead
make a clean sweep of them like this:

Tie on a raven's shaggy ruff, roll r's and
kraaaak kraaaak.

MANICHEANS

At the impassable end of beach
where the creek mouth, debris-wracked
sputters over slimy cobbles,
turkey vultures congregate
with their plucked, boiled faces, no-necked
heads ridiculous marbles on a 6 ft. span.

Untouchables at their melancholy chore,
chattel to carrion, labouring for the meat
that perisheth. Offal scoundrels, what is
their recompense? To love thee, garbage, more.
To delve deeper into detritus: rotten salmon,
washed up chopped seal.

Does their demeanor signify mortification?
Inarticulate, they squabble over tidbits,

turn from our reproach, loft off.
Two tones on the underside
of each wing; mud and cloud.
Diurnal dualists, they soar dihedral.
In flight, a loveliness far surpassing
that of swans. A contrariness
that endureth
to everlasting.

"THE LAW IN MY MEMBERS WARS AGAINST THE LAW OF MY MIND"

Dog scrapes a lush grass bed under the apple tree,
circles three times and dissolves in dappled shade.
Flaked out, muscles heat-slacked. Ants file unnoticed
over paws. Eyelids flutter. She drops
her guard, slides out of wakefulness
and is seduced by dreams.

And where will it end, all this living after the flesh?

Hard at my desk work,
I keep the body under. Resist
gazing at the dog's slaked rest.
Oh I am mortified! The duvet of drowsiness
steals over me. Who will save me
from this small delicious death?

Slowed breath. I enter the bower of naptime.
Careless as a pup, and carnal.

WHY PRAIRIE BARNS ARE RED

Potatoes, cod cakes, cauliflower.
Guests in the Abbey dining room mutter.
Blandness tastes like a personal slight,
a reduction in sophistication status.
They crave exotic condiments
to mask wholesomeness as thrilling
as the corn stubble horizon.

Maelstrom of gulls churns over calcareous fields
just turned. Grey mantles, black wing tips reeling.
Their lower mandibles, red-spotted.

Red as counterweight.

Do you want all of that red at once? Now?
Pour it down your discriminating throat?
Panic Red, Passion Red, Pope Red, Choke-
on-it Red.

Don't forget what the abased in Spirit get.

Circle of white-faced cattle, rattled by a juicy jackrabbit
that corrals them. The cows bellow off; the rabbit
sits down like a hummock
and disappears. A surfeit of grey counterpointed
by dots of barns
like low bush cranberries in pemmican.

When you're in Rome,
eat as the Romans eat ...
honeyed turnip, braised onions.
Slowly your eyes learn to savour what is set before them.

That way, Feast Days will practically blind you.

Today, Thanksgiving! Chokecherry wine and mead.
Sarsaparilla laces pumpkin pie the way
barns strut at dusk.

A LIGHT BURDEN

Clouds streak down the strait and settle
oomph on hill flanks. We propel ourselves
into vacation and wait to stabilize.
It involves long gazes over the bay
and much leaning into driftwood. Nights, our heads
loll about in sedges,
inquire after constellations.

The dog, always fully in her own body,
laps water from a deep bowl
without restraint.

In time, mind lets up on its labour, slips off
its cargo. Heavy laden, the known self eases up,
steps out of its burdens.

Green apples redden.
Under the tree, white wicker armchairs
issue invitations: from the shaded table
take up the open book, a cup.

Honeysuckle unfurls in hedges. Evenings,
our shoulders stroked
by their yoke of cream and nutmeg.

ADVENT FOLLY

Cirrocumulus torsade of peach-tinged pearls,
sunrise wreath above Gulf Islands where
perky grebes hurl themselves out of cerise water,
plunge and emerge grinning.

A stupendous drama: Something Big
is about to happen. Normally restrained
and law-abiding, morning sky loses
its better judgement, goes ultra purple.

So Incarnation breaks through: Myth into History.
Magic fuses with the ordinary
while firm-footed fir and sensible cedars scoff
at the dyed tumult.

Preposterous as herald angels,
carnadine skeins streak the apricot dawn.
Velvet painting offense
to the tasteful who prefer their miracles

toned down. Now shore waves turn so mauve
they embarrass reason. What to do
with this unbelievable story? Riotously
Advent assaults common sense.

THE GUADALUPE APPEARS TO
NIEMAN-MARCUS SHOPPERS IN ARIZONA

End of an arid spending day. Moment
for hills to blush; sun splinters a halo
through fan palms. Hush of roses.

Mall parking lots tinge peach. The super-rich
super-bored glance up, those dry glittery
Scottsdale women. Low-degree light slant

exalts rocks, a pink dew. Serras conté-edged.
Why do they not hold their breath,
the laméd matrons, for the way her sky cloak

shoulders her rhodonite robe starry with Christmas lights?
Her sunset heightened skin. They glance away,
pedicure perfect, designer dulled. Crevices

already muted and chill. Cinders. Birds mock.
The champagne blond women go grey. Here
was the gift for those who have everything; but …

ALONE IN THE HOUSE ON CHRISTMAS EVE
WITH THE BLESSED SACRAMENT

A naive nativity crèche
where wet muzzles of oxen nuzzle
divine pudgy feet. "Manger" as in "to eat", as in
this pretend bread, cradled here on the dining table
in a makeshift cereal bowl paten.

Vigil light invites me, awake at night
and discomfited, to come
and visit. I say, "Hello, are you there
Awake One?" An infant broken in bits
makes the smallest possible meal for the whole world.

I settle on the sofa.
Abandon myself to a circlet of unleavened wheat.
Safe as a newborn asleep
in the halo of mother love.

REVELATION

Lines of geese emerge onto the bay at dawn.
The young in lower case script bracketed
by capital adults. Ink serifs,
Alpha and Omega.

From where did it appear, this serene code?
Cowled in velour, hemlocks meditate on the shore.
From velvety cuffs, their long fingers
point out something.

Crows harass an eagle that wings away,
only the white fan rump visible in front
of flounced cedars. A vellum scrap,
it parts the dark forest screen, dissolves.

There are things revealed and those
which remain hidden. Search
along the shore for a creek mouth.
It eludes your will,

the coppery place draped with willow.
The geese return unscrolled;
importune them.

ADAM AND EVE IN MIDDLE AGE

CALLING

A cornucopia, this lane's hedge, until now.
Thimbleberries and tendrilled vetches tangled in filaree.
Little homes of the scurried. Cat's ears
and Ox-eye daisies bright in their constellations.

To prosper sprawled borders: for this
Adam and Eve were commissioned.
Nootka roses wafting, the subtle honeysuckle.
But today we round the corner and meet offence.

Gone the relaxed property lines of our neighbours.
Scraped, verges shaved and sanitized
by a fence. Gateless,
keeping nothing in or out.

We plan spray paint, slogans:
"Down with the Cult of Homogeneity!"
Called to preach the uncontainable, missionaries of mess.

Towhee on a fence post reclaims his territory, whining.
In our pockets, umbels of dried seed
wild rose cuttings, native berry canes.
Horn of disarray.

VALENTINE'S DAY

Heart-on-sleeve flashy blackbird,
freshly returned from a winter's celibacy,
acts like he owns the marsh.
Angry at my red scarf's challenge,

he scatters cordate call notes
curved to a taper, over the soggy sedges
ditches, horse-trails and wakes
dormant hormones in every stirring thing.

He doesn't dither. "I long I long I long,"
his plaint a struck gong. Is this flirting
or harassment? Neither, the way his voice
is neither song nor honk. The way sex

is not about sex. Why does he want the territory?
So that he can share it, press it
into foreverness. He dons gold-tasseled epaulets
of Eros, wings on fire for the reciprocity

that is about more than genitals, the insertion
of the penile shaft into the vaginal barrel.
At the top of a hawthorn he worries
his raw wound open, gilt-edged.

ASHES

Rubber-booted compost makers, we drag
slimy whips of kelp onto the gravel beach,
machete them in chunks. Rain engraves the bay.
Good weather to gather kelp; no observers out
with queries, to which I usually reply,
"potash, iodine, bug deterrent and better tomatoes".
And my husband adds, straight-faced,
"great with shrimp, tossed in a little oil".

A cluster of ragged poplars edges the shore.
In their tops, starlings imitate a struggle of leaves.
November storms have blown in a harvest of huge seaweed tangles
which glint offshore, camouflage loons.

Beach hoppers scavenge in knotted pyres
already going soft with rot. The hard holdfasts now belly-up,
grasp air.

A car drives up full of passengers
who stare past us at the water. Then another car
and a third. Sombre adults and awed children
in formal occasion clothes. Each carries a red flower.
One holds an ornate silver urn. The littlest girl
clutches a letter.

An older man asks if we would leave for a few minutes.
We clamber up rocks at the narrow mouth of the cove.
Our backs turned to them, we speak of our own favoured places,
stare out and grow silent. When we turn, they are leaving.
One of them waves to us.

Our feet crunch loudly on the gravel as we resume our task. Rain clatters.
Wet wisps of hair sting my eyes.
The machete sounds scales as it cuts down
water-filled lengths, resonant
as an underwater pipe organ. Roses
enmeshed in kelp, ebb out. Afloat among them
white notepaper folds open.

Let's pack it in. Enriched by wrack,
we go home and eat
the last tomatoes
from our fall garden.

SKINNYDIPPING

Hike to Little Sliamon Lake; easygoing at first
on old logging roads, then we cut off
and step up into hemlock forest. Narrow path,
unsure boulders slippery with dry needles.
We miss the sights for fear of tripping;
eyes intent on the next step.

The dog, squirrel chaser, bear sniffer,
takes the bluffs at double speed, unthinking.

Descend and blue lake threads appear
between cedar trunks. Clambering down
Kinnikinnick matted cliffs, we learn quick caution
around juniper. Consult a ponderous field guide
about Salish staple berries.

Take out sketchbooks. Figure out the pattern
of conifers at a distance; lattice of dark diamonds
outlined with feather light. Didn't get it.
Try again.

A loon lumbers three heavy circles above
the too-small lake before ascent;
efforts to let go of effort.

Timid, we undress, worry about duck mites
and slide into silt. Merged with tepid water
toil dissolves.

Against the peaty shore
slup slup
water tongues suck hickeys.

REDBREASTED MERGANSERS
for F.W. on her fiftieth

Unmated females hang around the creek mouth.
It is July; too late for breeding. The rakish males off north
with younger mates, showing off, rearing more offspring.

But these, exempt, just want to have fun. Ovulation's over,
no squabbling young. They skitter in surf, chase breakers, run.
There's no alarm. No harsh *karr* sounds of the breeding grounds.
They fish in small groups. Afternoons, a communal preen,
then leave for evening events in sedate rows.
Return much later, a straggly line. Inebriated string
of rhodonite pebbles.

Post-menopausal friends around oval dining tables,
around workshops, hot tubs. Seaside, funny side.
Your guard dropped with your fertility.
Ribald with relief, birds of a feather, grey-crested, maturely lumped.
We eat prawns, a little sushi; dive confidently
for confessions. I am strung
on this necklace of semi-precious stones,
set in this circlet. Flock, rufous with affection,
cackling.

MT. TRAUBERG

On the cupola apex, cumuli gather and explode.
The mountain calls clouds to itself, escarpments
seduce storms. Forest flanks elope with bluffs,
a northwest marriage of cover and exposure
frequently overcast, where the principal vegetation
is moist disarray.

We did effort once to ascend it, this nondescript bump
on the log of the coast. After all these years
ridges, plateaus still newly revealed by cloud shade,
lifted up by low slanted light. Sometimes
I swim out into the strait to glance back at it,
shyly, see it more elevated.

How do you decipher a mountain let alone
paraphrase it? I still need a field guide
for the common species of marital emotions.
Understand it? Hike the logging road
of causality and end up on a clear cut.
The mountain keeps its inscrutable troth.

Storm blasts stone-sized rain through the screen
onto the gentle card you sent for our anniversary.
"Two paths joined," it says, till rain runs with ink,
washes words. I slide the chill door shut.
Our lives gather, diverge
and we start over.

Why did we strain so? Where we have settled now,
on Trauberg's rainy foot, we look out
on easy sails that slip along the horizon. Emerald breakers
draw themselves up and disperse
over boulders clustered round the turquoise rim.
Zillions of diatoms sparkle and often
we laugh for no reason.

A MIDDLE-AGED COUPLE GOES TO THE BEACH TO NECK

So windy, windsurfers cower back to shore;
congregate like black ants.

A freighter flounders on the strait;
pilot boat plumes out to its side.

You light up a smoke inside your coat
and almost put yourself on fire.

I shriek like a gull.
This is about tearing off insulation,

bodies unnumbed
by the numbing wind.

We open beer behind logs,
poke our reckless heads over.

Blundering out of harbour in a storm
to reclaim what has gone adrift.

"...AND WHATEVER ADAM CALLED EVERY LIVING THING, THAT WAS THE NAME THEREOF"

Pats of butter
on a green twig shelf.
Sun melts them open.					*Broom*

New fronds unfurl,
paws of shy animals
coppery fur.					*Bracken*

Geodesic silk eiderdowns
float on a bed of quills.					*Dandelion*

Plain bridesmaids
piled up giggly
group glamour.					*Saskatoons*

Green bulbous hearts shiny
among brown flowerets
crisp as dried flies.					*Lilac*

EVE TELLS STORIES

Stray nasturtiums sprawl   *Convent Garden*
(Sister Immaculata's)
over compost piles.

Juncoes skittish   *Back From Summer*
black flash white fall.

Falling hail and slosh; a golden   *Yellow Tulip*
still intact étude
of Trinity; light with
its three-pommelled pistil
thank you.

Rooted bracken croziers   *Episcopal Convention*

Up in the green-draped   *Honeysuckle Minstrels*
musicians' gallery
fanfare! Brasses raised
at imprecise angles
but raised and pointed more or less up
Cheeks puffed. Hark!

CONJUGAL RELATIONS

We shift back and forth on slippery concrete
draw together and apart, miss serves,
connect badly, my spouse and I
playing third-rate tennis in the rain
laughing because no one is here to watch us.
Amateurs, we pretend to be good, while
we are so inept, which doesn't matter.
Volley insults at each other
and compliments
seldom finish a set
the court littered with balls
take lots of breaks without blame
threaten to quit
come home an hour late elated
having stumbled on the elixir of love
mutually sweaty
and inadequate.

But when I show you this poem
you get a little huffy
like the first time I brought home vitamins
specially formulated for seniors.

Sovereign remedy: the game
of cherishing flaws.

Okay, I take it back.
You are great at tennis.

BACKBONE AND FOREBODING

On flaccid yellow stems, fall tomatoes fatten,
red as the Queen of Hearts and confident.
Yet vines are more stricken every morning
and brittle leaves shrink. Dowagers who diminish
as calcium leaches from fused vertebrae.

The garden dejects itself with thoughts
of the compost pile while in its midst
glowing fruit plumps up and preens.
Who allows you to escape
from the wrath to come?

Too late for stems slouched against
their cages. Too late for chiropractor
and chiropodist. Overnight, slumped
skeletons vanish, (cancel the orthopod)
while red globes light up like Christmas.

We stand in the evening garden and rip
defiant fruit from ropy branches,
suck reckless juices. Washing my hands
in the white enamel sink, I rub at brown spots
lately settled among scrawny veins.

The stained sink brilliant
with lime green juice.

HYAKATAKE

Struck dumb
by a Love Like This which comes but once
in a thousand years. Solemnly
we gather to court the comet or at least
the idea of comet. Tugged from dull sofas
we stand in awe on beaches, hilltops
turn from city lights and fall
for this sight. Necking.

Myth of Romance buzzes like sparklers on a cake.
Our selves enlivened! Willing victims
of this Thing that is Bigger than us,

a chunk of dirty ice circling our star.
Its tail evaporation like the kettle whistling.
Some carbon monoxide, sunlight's reflection
on fluorescent gases. A hundred widths of the moon
in length. The moon

behind our backs, predictable Luna snug to Earth.
The earthshine moon, old in the new moon's arms.
So common at dusk when we drive home, we've grown
accustomed to it as to pot roast and the evening news.

And sometimes low in the west, conjoint Venus.

TO THE SAME WINDOW AGAIN

Late March hills astonish themselves
with fresh snow. They look in the mirror
and get a kick. Skyline draws itself
with a fine frost nib. How do you live
in your own common place as if
you visit it for the first time? How to walk
down your own driveway and see it
with fresh eyes like a trip to Alaska
or a just-discovered Rembrandt etching?

Some worried bird is always tut tutting
in tenacious birches. Open the fridge
and perfume of cantaloupes smacks you in the face.
Wow. A soft rush! After decades, how
to start a new marriage with a long-time spouse?
Burn the dividing screen that commemorates wars
and carve a reredos of peace? The moon
is a hard pencil crescent;
the moon is a silver canoe.

How do you slip into familiar clothing
and invite a different persona?
That lift. That felt shift in being,
like a yellowed shirt, bleached.
Surprise yourself: look out
the same window you look out of every morning
at another angle. Hear yourself repeat
the lines of a worn script, then
stop repeating.

On the radio, a song you distrust
catches you off guard. Surrender
to the same window, look out.
Notice you begin to cry.

FIVE LENTEN EXERCISES

i
Okay, draw something simple
like this garden chair. Draw it
so you could sit on it
more or less. A first lesson
in crooked humble sitting.

ii
Here is the teapot and bowls.
Paint the teapot with five brushstrokes,
the bowls with two. Then
do something easy
like the twenty-six steps
to pour tea.

iii
The dog's spirit quickens
with the whiff of squirrel
or dull drop of catkin on moss.
Let her tutor you. Alert yourself
to maple flowers, the scent
of jade water.

iv
Five driftwood planks: solid bench
under the green-pricked ocean spray hedge.
Now practice reverie which encompasses
choppiness.

v
Confine your palette. Reduce
the bay to its essence; similarly
restrict yourself to this
breath, this monohued now.

EVERY POLARITY ATTRACTS ITS OPPOSITE

Starling horde infects the oak meadow.
Fevered whistles, a whirring workshop
full of clicks, fan belts needing oil.

Tiresome birds who appear to neither
toil nor reap nor keep Lent. To those
who espouse simplicity is given

frantic companions. Hermit heckled
with hooting. Rookery droppings abound
on the ascetic. They catcall, deride

penitence, these lice-ridden rags
of sparkling cloisonné.

EMPTYING THE HANDS

Distrust prophets who sound good.
Bury your face in the froth of *Prunus* petals
splattered on wet pavement. Do not listen
to soothsayers who soothe. God stands aloof;
in Lent you get used to it. And anyway,
who can live with consuming fire?
Retreat from heat; enter the March mountain air,
the long cold back of Lent.

Pin oaks reach straight out for a smatter
of good news, claws of spent leaves clutch on.
Clouds busy themselves hauling slate.

The city preens. Ponds and lakes glitter:
the craving to be clean crossed
with the yearning for rich things.
To the west, Cascades, acres of ice,
gleam like scrubbed pewter plates holding bread.

Eat it slowly. When the hands are full
of grasping, how do they open?

Cherry blossoms pelt, are crushed by traffic.
Steeled against temptation, trudge
the astringent street of a sparse self.

The forty days draw themselves
with a few ink strokes.
Hunger for hunger satisfied.

THE SILENCE THAT IS NOT SILENCE AT ALL

Unobtrusive as dawn, the lake balances perfectly
between East and West. An early hiker
rounds the corner, headset clamped on.

Juncoes *tsk tsk* and give way. Starlings catcall.
Merganser, all white hood, skims
a straight arrow line, alights with a velvet swoosh
pursues prey through clear water
soundless.

Lichen-stained alders circle the shore,
haloed with smudges of alizarin catkins.   *Red dye*
Aments upon aments. A lent retreatant, I come
for the annual fast from stimulation,
rededicate to silence or at least
to the diminishment of stimulants.

Make way for tumult. Here are the Big Ego geese.
Indignant honking, they want to be noticed.
Chest beating, a squall of identity.

LONG WEEKEND ON MAYNE ISLAND

> *"Yet a little sleep, a little slumber,*
> *a little folding of the hands to sleep."*
> Book of Proverbs

Drowsy as a monotone, dreary as uillean pipes
weather tears away our plans.
(A day to picnic on the shore, a day to hike the bluffs,
and one more to sketch the lighthouse.)

Rain mullions decks. Fog drones. Island hills
erase themselves. Lulled by indoor comforts,
dulled days pass entranced. Bleary as the windows,
we doze.

At Georgina Point, the crisp lighthouse
straightens itself, a tall white gate open
into Active Pass, red trim sharp as a siren.

> *I will go there now, on chill glacier stripped rocks-*
> *where drenched arbutus shine naked*
> *beside the lacy droop of cedars.*
> *I will wake now —*
> *my black lab prances around me*
> *sifting water scents, spicy gull droppings.*
> *I crunch the gravel path, carry my watercolours .*
> *up the slope of the lighthouse keeper's neat lawns.*

But here, indoors, all is entrenched
in half-sleep thick as a headache.

> *In the channel, gulls saunter, are stirred,*
> *paper cinders on a whirl.*
> *Water tenses up for the wrestle*
> *between tides; spasms in a narrow pass.*
> *The beacon is clarion fierce*
> *a wrench of alarm.*

Through hypnagogia's murk my arm reaches for,
touches, a shred of wakefulness, falls back,
seduced by slumber's parching potion.

Three whole days, thirsty for that lit lantern,
each time I surface from sleep with proverbs:
"who lies in woeful state..." and
"behold, the bridegroom cometh".

SHOPLESS IN SEATTLE

Stunned panhandler fronts the tasteful shop
where I pick through stuff designed
to camouflage privilege; dark-hued clothes
with wrinkled castoff looks, bad pottery,
chic lumpy glass wrapped in rough paper fashionably
tied with straw. *Au naturel,* as the puffy upturned palm
of this scab-faced, torn-blanketed
undisguised beggar.

Disturber sir, your presence drains my pleasures.
Awkward cipher I cannot erase. Ash Wednesday
to my Easter. You are a discord
in the hummable tune of prosperity, the rust
I cannot polish away.

Around the unkempt parking lot, weedy vines
shoot out furled green fans still pleated moist
from tight beginnings. Along serrated leaf edges,
blemished indents, insect-chewed before
they've fully opened.

The imposition of the ashes on my forehead
leaves a greasy smudge.
Repentance, the rubric says
for stains within.

ST. BASIL'S UKRANIAN CHURCH

A string of pearls flung out
and there are snow geese.

Floppy snowflakes wander hasty as a chant,
circumnambulate, forget where they are going.
Orthodoxy of snow; a harmony
with what encompasses. Floes of flakes, semitonal,
on the surface of invisible rivers which shift
backwards and forwards. Each flake surrenders
its original self, becomes pointless as plainsong.

To wander, a mendicant, the doxology on your lips.
Snow on your tongue. Heat emits from your palms.
Sometimes your throat breaks open.
Now the cantor lisps almost falsetto.
A prayer you recognize
in a language you do not understand.

To be chant in the world. Morning and evening
to submit to snow. To learn its humming.
Forty days you do service in the stubble
on your bare feet and for your reward,
a red osier.

A LENT RETREATANT TRAVELS HOME

Mountain angels imprint their wings
on snow up there in *kairos*, glacier time.
Down on the Puget Sound, triangles of white gulls
flutter their *chronos* coverts, circumnavigate
the Strait.

Tides calculate Foulwater Bluff, Marrowstone Island.
Ferries crisscross briskly and the coast is full
of old defenses. Above is constancy.
Above, silver hurricanes devise a feather geometry.
Nothing hurries ice.

Sun, moon, stars wheel over inclined ranges
and pitched roofs of miniature shore houses
where absorbed children play in sand.
Warp and woof. Two worlds,
this ticking one and that Olympic one timeless as stone.

Children play at the loom that binds both,
can teach you citizenship in both nations.
Remember Everest's summit is marine limestone.
Stand up, shake snow off your sleeves;
you approach the jagged international boundary.

SUPPOSING HIM TO BE THE GARDENER

Pendant maple racemes descend lime green above
the abandoned trolley track I call a trail,
minutes from the highway,
a sequestered dell.

On the first day of the week
very early in the morning.

Birches beaded with crystal catkins.
My old black lab lit up
with a million pinpricks of fine rain.

Who is it you are looking for?

Song sparrow on a perch,
a shadow-streaked chest,
dark confluence. Who
do I seek.
My knee bends
in a vale of fawn lilies swaying
on their slender stems:
strips of linen
carefully folded.

Maestro, gardener.

All things
in heaven and earth bow down.

Wild grape hyacinths clutched to my vest
gather a purple stain.

INTO THE CLEARING

EMILY DICKINSON

White hawthorn on the edge of the clearing,
boughs dusted with blossoms,
armfuls of powder,
makes no effort
to take a stance.

Luscious laburnum brags in its confident place.
Mature arbutus, maples used to their roles,
position themselves with experience.

The hawthorn looks unfinished, her naive leaves
play skip. The flowers are nondescripts
and know it.

To be naked is the way of safety.
To be disarmed is to be ready.

The hawthorn folds herself to the light,
steps forward, enters into the presence
of the clearing. Without pleas,
without solutions, just as she is.

PUBESCENCE

January alders thrust out catkins;
citric green on one side and the other
rust red. Cheeky show-offs

do they respect their crotchety elders,
previous generation strobiles
a sprig higher?

You know how it is. There you are
walking along mildly depressed
and used to it

when you notice their strut.
Gangly adolescents with bad complexions.
They're making all the noise.

They're the only juice around
and they know it. Limbs askew, they dismiss
last year's crones who just hang on

by a thin thread, muttering.

COVENANT

Mild in their manner
but resolute

field daffodils emerge, dare to say yes
just yes

that's all
not the noise of debate

not the hothouse of opinion
just yes

the power of those
who are sure of their season

though the mornings of thick darkness
are not yet past.

THE PRIESTESS ROLE OF A BOTANICAL ILLUSTRATOR

Snap the lacquered hyacinth stem; it spits juice.
The bronze buds are propped-up miniature vases,
tight-lipped, a few flirty ith mauve tips. Cross-section them.
Next, crack open a daffodil, split sideways
the dirndle of fused petals, confuse the calyx and tear open
the papery sheath with your fingernail. Now
some sloping crocuses, mouths agape. Accept no hesitations,
slice them right down their saffron tongues. Try to razor open
the chestnut bud. No use, so sketch the whole sticky specimen.
(That's a job no thin-point pen could describe: only charcoal
can swirl and pleat this in-your-face insolence.)
As for the maple pendulums, sway
as you draw those ponds of pollen cupped in your palm.
Divide the specimens on the frost-tinged moss. Walk
between the halves and draw up this document.

> *Let me be split thus and worse*
> *exposed to ice, predator mosquitoes, probing creepers*
> *should I forget, should I fail*
> *to notice the covenant of incipience.*
> *Let dread fall on me and nightmares,*
> *should I cease to celebrate unstoppable Eros.*

Sun as it sets slants through the mist. Moist air
falls down like smoke.

Forsythias twinkle, a host of uncountable stars.
Stand under tasseled alders, their strobiles too tough to split.
Tap them. A shower of notched discs,
enclosed seed grains, multitudinous as sand.

Daffodil trumpets blow in a new moon.

SPRING SALAD

A mallard drake skitters over the pond on drunken water-skis.
The hen outflaps him, stays just
ahead of her pursuer with hairpin twists. When she succumbs
she does so utterly, disappears from sight.
He mounts her here on the patio by our feet, he mounts her there
under the picnic table. This is not cherry blossoms.
But then, quietude. She resumes dabbling. He rattles his butt a bit,
waddles off, the neck-biter.

On a monotonous day, sudden forsythias appear,
their noses squashed against the window. Hyperactive children
who cannot be calmed by disapproval.

Catkins stutter. The precocious osoberry reeks of urine;
cat pee to be exact. Bushtits palpitate in droves.

Yet one particular evening, probably in March,
when maples toss lime green confetti
and deer swaying on their hind legs nibble
drooping racemes their front hooves pull down...
and robins call in a timbre as distinct
as the scent of first-mown grass ...
a passage opens in the throat of the listener
who nuzzles into the woods
to pick the spring ephemerals
for a purslane salad,
pretty as candy with a taste of pond.

POOR CLARES

Overwhelmed by lilacs' bombast
and bragging rhododendrons, who
would note these drab flowers
so insignificant even the field guides
omit a mention?

Yellow beaded tassels of Garry Oak;
though botanically correct,
you'd hardly call them flowers.

You could look straight at them and not see;
bump into them and feel nothing.
Miniature cascades of tufted rope
arch out from under leaf buds. Cenobites
so self-effacing
only true observers pay attention.

Rows of tiny knotted cords, unobtrusive
but not wimpy. Ostentatious as sand.
Indigent, utterly spared
of illusion about florist shops, exotics
in hothouses.

Everyone knows acorns' shallow scaly cups,
pocketed by toddlers, mealy fruit chewed
by squirrels, band-tailed pigeons, even humans
in great need of edibles. How is it
the lobed leaves are as familiar
as nuns' habits, yet

so few find the narrow way?

MAGNOLIAS

emerge from husks, slant tiptoe
on slim twigs and simulate stars.

Flutter of wings askew,
a generosity of white.

Girls at their first communion,
innocence made more so, unaware

as they are, of the odd barbed cone
nascent bulbous mound,

its shocking hot pink seed.

MANNA

This spring I get more stuck in whining.
At the same time, more struck
by arbutus trees in flower.
Trunks rusty as robins' breasts
clucking contentment.

Madronas are crowned with snowy clusters
of milky miniature urns. Shy lilies-of-the-valley
multiplied skyward. Are they more profuse now
than ever before or is my eye
more eager for a sign, greedy for comfort?
Arranged in round collars of brisk glossy leaves,
bouquets for all spring brides. Plenty enough
to toss to every hopeful girl, hands raised
to catch.

Walk out into the May night
under a canopy of noiseless bells
and inhale honey. Slow down
breath and eyes. See the ground
strewn like hoarfrost.
You are provided for.
Exhale your litany of murmurings
easily as this fall of creamy nectar.
Gather it up.

MEMBRANOUS SPACE IN INFANT'S HEAD
AT ADJACENT ANGLES OF PARIETAL BONES
for Marianne

Implausible as peacocks in a northwest fog,
hydrangeas unfold their baby blue miniature fists. Just at the point
when miscarriage stuffs your soul into a place too small for it,
just when you drain away into the captivity of loss,
hydrangeas repeat a small word about the way
you might touch your own pain as you would stroke a fontanel.
Hydrangeas have flown to the tropics and stolen azure sky scraps
to line a little coffin. Gaze at the veins of these petals;
what pulses there without protection.

DOWAGERS

Gossamer wrinkles on throats, lips;
tulips in decline get more peculiar.
Overfussed frills.
Quavery fear of falling
into disarray.

But they hang on impossibly
one more day. Insist
on one more appearance.

Lustrous, one petal outshines the others;
its twisted tips a brittle lace.

Quivers whisper over draped skin.

HYPO-THYROID WALTZ

Robust as fiddlers' jigs, June erupts
from conifer tips, jolts out of arbutus crowns.
Lime-green June turns rock cliffs into gardens,
lines ditches with nests of ferns, mixes
yellows and greens on an island palette.
Overwhelmed by verdure,

I stand beneath a Grand Fir, try to inhale
its health. Tiers upon tiers of needles splay out;
green fringed shawls of flamenco dancers.
Latticed branches glisten with the sweat of zeal.
Endocrine-depleted, gland- fatigued, I back off. Too fragile
for exuberance, unsure of what my synapses crave,

ramble down a gravel track and receive
the missing nutrient: Nootka roses in a meadowful dose.
They drizzle fragrance. Upturned faces
a delicate balance of naturopathic pinks. We are
so easily bruised, so quickly out of step
in hormones' complex dance. But here

(raucous greens calm down) a laying on of petals
restores the desire to waltz.

MORNING, NOON AND NIGHT

Full of enterprise, finches
carpet the thicket with twitters,
cacophony of busyness.

All the hot midday, red-eyed towhees
whine in the dust,
spoilt children.

Flicker high in oak labyrinths
exults. Sunrise under one wing,
its going down under another.

HERMIT'S GARDEN

She weaves from shade to light and back,
tends her patch of herbs
some straggly for want of Mediterranean heat
some happy as prayers. Deer are welcome
to take what they need. Frail shoots are netted.
Some things need coaxing, some neglect.

The inner order twins the outer.
She concentrates her solitude on a row she calls Rwanda.
The patch of Kosovo she shields from frost
with her own clothes. By the gate
a bed of Palestine nurtured with water
she carries from the creek.

Deprivation and merriment grow together;
silence and jubilation go hand in hand.

Her garden cultivates concord.
Every metre set right. World worker,
anchorite of the cosmos, she casts
her love on the receiving winds;
it changes the invisible habitants of the air.

ECOFEMINIST THEACOSMOLOGY

Orb weaver coasts down from heaven
on her secret thread, pendulums across
the clearing, wafts past at eye-level
floats back and encircles me
in a dawdle. What
is the object of her silk gaze?
Matter is energy moving in defined patterns
of relation; the very small
with the very large. But
all explanations are partial.
At dusk, sun reverses the known,
fills the void with slanted light.
Willows, crow's nest and me
all connected. The whole clearing
and its verges touched with galaxies
of lit-up filament. Is there a centre,
manifest? It is
everywhere.

PAVAROTTI TAKES WATERCOLOUR LESSONS

Evening inches toward the river;
drop a little blue into willows.

Bleached sedges on the bank go slack;
rub lightly with a sponge.

Humble with a little grey the alders
pretending to be evergreens.

Cedars regale the riverside with aristocracy
but times are tough; touch them with rust.

Then daub yellows on the fine edged stencils
of maple hands.

Last the sumac in full feather. It takes
the whole palette. Toss

an entire opera of colour
onto that peacock.

THIEVES

A rain of robins in arbutus crowns, drunk
on fruit dyed the riot of sunset. I crane
Open-mouthed, steal time to stare.

Peach-breasted birds shower noise, a downpour.
Berries drop, bounce off hard ground
into shrubbery. Now the concourse whooshed away

by the hint of a goshawk
still far off
like the threat of drought.

SETTING FIRE TO THE EARTH

Chlorophyll exits from the stage.
Autumnal equinox ablaze with xanthophyll!
Leaves exalt themselves. Banners unfurl
in bottomlands. Hill slopes rigged out,
a garish fair. The glades full
of their own performance.
Grand finale in meadows.

Soon the pageant flags
flutter brown; high-flyers abased.
In the wings, worms
the lowly ones who have their meal
and release it to roots.

So long anthocyanin, farewell abscission.
Some sugar pulls the curtain down
and goes off with an old starch.

Long after the applause dies down,
humus uses embers. Fire kindled
in the earth, all ready.

THE ESCHATOLOGY OF WOE AND
THE ESCHATOLOGY OF BLISS

Plate-sized leaves of maple *macrophyllum*
spiral down. Now some of these amber sky-divers
parachute on to the driveway.
They collapse colour, dissolve into
tramped mud.
Others, flying yellow ponchos
saunter into the rockery where no one steps on them
but when the sun shrivels out
they curl up in fetal position and crumble.
Still others gold rimmed, green veined
and young looking skip down and impale themselves
on holly, hang there choking.
But many there are in all colours and sizes
who descend onto the vegetable bed. To humus
they return. And what riches will be revealed
from this balsam-scented mould?
A hundredfold.
Now if you have ears to hear
you may deduce meaning,
secure a precise application such as
the cultivation of strong cabbages and onions.
But if you have a heart, weep.
For this is about waste.
Waste. Endless profligate, big-leafed heaven,
spends as it pleases, claims this is
all for the best.
Autumn extravagant gone mad.

AVIAN THERAPY

Pert juncos, skittish finches
gather around feeders, litter
deck and railings with millet husks,
seed chaff. Wind

winnows leftovers. I count
sparrows in the hedge, name them
song, white crowned, vesper.
It gentles me, avian therapy.

But do they care for me?

Goshawk perched in a warped oak
picks at feathered clumps under her talons.
I stare with binoculars, she stares back. Brazen.
I am nervous as a flicker.

WATERSHED

Purple/blue salmon backs arch themselves up the river.

Caution, the sign says, *Active Hauling,* as if
we could not read the signs around us
here in timber country
where no attempt is made
to prettify the industry of the place.

A logging truck careens past
and leaves unscathed a muddy newt,
its underside an orange intense
as new cut cedar.

We count culverts, dawdle at a slough.
Mallard hens grunt their clarinets, heave
from slate pebbles into clay water.
Their brilliant red feet as startling as ornamental carp.

Lime green moss clutches maple trunks.
Leaves yellow down; slow motion fans
waft on surveyors' fluorescent pink tapes
beside saplings spray-painted
with scribbled numbers
and *timber sale, fall boundary.*

But here along a small creek,
the bright sign we hoped to find:
Riparian Reserve Zone

WHAT YOU HAVE ALWAYS WITH YOU

Sapsucker, rapid knocker
on dull wood,
flashes her jeweled head.

Under the cover of laurels,
shy fox sparrows do their trot
intent on the meal
beneath their feet
making a waltz out of hunger.

Saskatoon berry bushes—fruitless
on this too wet coast—
festooned with bunched rubies,
native honeysuckle berries draped
over their barren host.

Blessed are you who make loveliness
from nothing. Blessed are you
when you borrow without shame.
You who know your need for beauty,
so that you may live, and being poor
must find it anywhere.

Unripe clumps of blackberries
silver with mould beside
a ribbed riot of purple veins,
leaves wine-tipped.

SANTA RITA ABBEY

WHO IN THEIR RIGHT MIND

Summer constellations up in the March sky.
  Pre-dawn air fragrant with lilies where
  there are no lilies.

Off to vigils with a flashlight,
  tithe on the night's deep sleep.
  Returning a portion from whence it came.

This is for real; people really do this
  for a living. Rise in the middle of dreams
  to pay rapt attention to a flickering candle.

Someone, somewhere on earth is doing this
  at every moment. Who? Romantics, novices,
  insomniacs, owlers.

In their right mind, they stumble into dim chapels,
  discard sleep and slip into wakefulness.
  Alert and at ease in a different dream.

DESERT CISTERCIANS DECIDE TO PLANT ROSES

Coyotes yip in the gulch
    take to their heels at sun-up.
    They skulk past freshly planted rose stalks.
    Pruned down hard, the thorny stubs redolent
    of soft-edged ideas.

In the asperity of this place (hill wind howling,
    concrete soil) a convergence
    of identities: English Country Garden
    crossed with the whitened skull of Sonora.

I crave a single persona, come
    to these Catholic Quakers, hungry
    for the luxury of stasis, of fixed boundaries.

Why must simplicity's disciples wed adornment?
    Let the Strict Observers refuse compromise.

In the wash, cattle tracks cross the dirt road.
    One way goes the way of the rule-maker.
    The other is the way of the rule-breaker.

Pick up that crux and carry it.

Flycatchers rollercoaster into the gully
    backlit by sunset, ash-throated.
    Their tumbledown path intersects
    but does not hinder
    blithe coyotes who slink into dusk.

THE PRACTICE OF STANDING STILL

Under desert rock slabs, a spring gurgles,
   chitters over stones
   pastel as Easter eggs.

Moisture-seeking birds, Phoebes flit at the fountain
   lighter than dew
   than shade wisps of dry grass.

My approach as delicate as adobe.
   They vanish, reappear as plump fruit
   on mesquite.

I try to move like gauze drapes.
   Water sprays on my face, droplets
   cling to hair.

Santa Francisca, my palms fill with water;
   open to receive a wallop of warm feathers,
   the shock of trust.

THE SOLEMNITY OF JOSEPH

Walk to the hill, decide to climb,
Fifty-year-old body humbled.
At the top, a predictable whitened cattle skull
with the requisite royal-blue lupine
growing through it.

Make a sketch of the foothills. Lean against
a one-seed juniper and reconsider
the little silver-roofed abbey in the distance.

Not really being part of it; along for the ride.

Those virgins so wrapped up in holiness
they're pregnant with it.

Joseph, saint of aging women, you offered
a cloak of normalcy, protection to the ones
you could have turned your back on.
When you woke from your hilltop theophany
you consented to a walk-on part.

Steady patron, teach me to sit on sidelines,
a witness, content with my place
in the bigger picture.

Resinous juniper orchards spread over
rocky plateaus. Soft with bloom
sweet berry-like cones surround
their single seed.

FROM MY YOUTH THEY HAVE AFFLICTED ME
BUT NOT PREVAILED

Verdigris gecko, mini-tyrannosaurus, emerges
   from terracotta roof tiles, surveys baked adobe
   returns to curved shade.

Grass on the roof is slaving away.
   For what? It will never be grazed
   by lowing longhorn. Work ethic confounded,
   no one will gather it for seed or hay.

Heat ploughs the roof in furrows but
   to no avail. The sun a tyrant who abhors
   inner and outer nothing-doing.

Straw fades to white threads. In the ramada
   shade consoles me, unyoked
   from the noon weight of labour.

Pressed hard from my youth, but not destroyed.
   Weighed down but not withered.
   Grass blows away but breezes
   bless me in sheaves.

FLUFF

There are no easy sweets in the sparse chapel.
No friendly chorus, mood altering hymnlet.

The Scriptures are read stark as bare mesquite
in the gulch where raptors exult over rabbits.

It's all white chant. The air
from the foothills fringed with frost.

Beside the altar on Palm Sunday, a red vase of poppies.
My eyes fall on it ravenous.

Scraggly forsythia at the abbey entrance cower
beside spiny chollas fierce with yellow fruit.

Grey the drought-struck oaks: lance leaves
rough as emery. Fluff? In the gully, a ruined coyote,

poisoned probably. Clumps of belly fur feather out
and the reddish tail plumes, wind stroked.

ENCOMPASSED

All afternoon tramping unbroken range land
  around the abbey, my gait broken only
  by occasional cattle guards and stops
  to sip a water bottle.

Hoping for some rapture, a vision:
  shamanic bird, white wolf who speaks.
  Barring that, a bone scraper or stone pestle.

Soon all gulches start to look the same.
  Ascend an agave slope to get my bearings
  and foothills unroll, slow ziggurats.*
  There is the chapel spire and in each direction
  mountain ranges erupt from the desert floor,
  piles of giant arrowheads.

Return with a white dome of headache.

All night a slideshow of Southwest designs,
  coral and turquoise, sugelite and lapis
  The zigzags might be pyramid temple steps,
  lightning bolts or eagle wings outspread.

I join terracotta triangles, round the squares,
  set them inside ochre suns. Fix the directions,
  am gathered from four corners
  into the sanctuary of a dot.

Just before waking, add the fifth and sixth arrows:
heavenward and earth-centered.

*Ancient Assyrian or Babylonian temple in the form of a pyramid of terraced towers.

They live by bread, these Cistercians
that is, the daily baking of altar bread,
a *wholesome food product*. Over 300 parishes
purchase it in six different sizes
by UPS.

A hefty whole wheat whack-in-the-mouth
first meal, "most important" of the day.
With a strong swig of muscatel
you could survive on it.

And the Names they call this bread!
Saviour, Centre, Sacrifice.

When their baking day is done,
the sisters gather for vespers, gaze on
their substance, livelihood.

Through the east window, aloft
in a blue monstrance, wool-mottled moon.
A wafer you could call a lamb. That size
could be broken in five thousand pieces.

Phone or fax for free samples.

BAJADAS

"... knowing everything, rejecting nothing..."
Merton at Polonnaruwa

Gully, gulch, coulee, canyon. Folds in the drape
   of foothills that curve over earth's haunches
   then slope to the desert floor in slow motion scallops.

North-facing oaks and junipers pleat
   with south-loving agaves, cacti. Mesquite
   in the washes, an occasional white-boned willow.

A monotony full of potential, recumbent
   as oceans. Every wavelet a different shade of sage
   that shifts like colours on too-wet paper.

Content in themselves, foothills refute nothing,
   take no doctrinaire stance. Enormous reclined Buddhas,
   they discount nothing.

Clouds soften their bellies, take slow breaths.
   The bajadas are not the Higher Self, not the Lower.
   They are what you receive when discourse stops.

And their effusion is that of dry sycamores.
   Seed heads rustle; dancers with deer-hoof anklets.
   Beyond shadow, beyond disguise.

COMPLINE

For my father, of whom my mother said, "Death did him no harm".

Mauve-floored clouds cast shade lakes
   onto the desert floor. Lakes rise
   into the hills, cover whetstone mountains.

Bells ring last rite of the day. Verdin scatter
   in savanna grass, settle invisible
   in the shelter of shadows. No foot will tread on them.

How long does it take for eyes to adjust as day pales?
   White primroses tuft rocky slopes, open
   this evening for the first and only time.

Compline moths, sleeves to the knees, blanched unison
   in the unlit chapel, icon-drawn:
   the light of its countenance.

It takes as long as sleep's flutter. Shielded
   in feathers, fortressed by pinions:
   a safe and perfect end.

ACKNOWLEDGEMENTS

I am grateful to Charles Douglas, Tim Lilburn, and Susan McCaslin for their insightful reading and suggestions,

to Bob Soper and Wendy Nelems at Argonauta on Mayne Island for sharing their refuge,

to Al Grenier, my patient computer tutor, and

to Peggy Vanbianchi, artist, for permission to use "Wind Prayer"; to Jane Lindley, photographer of the boat; and to the Canadian Craft Museum where it was displayed.

H. M-vdK